DISCARD

Woodbourne Library
Washington-Centerville Public Library
Centerville, Ohio

P9-ASH-807

HOCKEY'S G.O.A.T.

WAYNE GRETZKY, SIDNEY CROSBY, AND MORE

JON M. FISHMAN

Lerner Publications ◆ Minneapolis

SCORE BIG with sports fans, reluctant readers, and report writers!

Lerner Sports is a database of high-interest biographies profiling notable sports superstars. Packed with fascinating facts, these bios explore the backgrounds, career-defining moments, and everyday lives of popular athletes. Lerner Sports is perfect for young readers developing research skills or looking for exciting sports content.

LERNER SPORTS FEATURES:

☑ Keyword search
☑ Topic navigation menus
☑ Fast facts
☑ Related bio suggestions to encourage more reading
☑ Admin view of reader statistics
☑ Fresh content updated regularly
and more!

Visit LernerSports.com **for a free trial!**

Copyright © 2020 by Lerner Publishing Group, Inc.

All rights reserved. International copyright secured. No part of this book may be reproduced, stored in a retrieval system, or transmitted in any form or by any means—electronic, mechanical, photocopying, recording, or otherwise—without the prior written permission of Lerner Publishing Group, Inc., except for the inclusion of brief quotations in an acknowledged review.

Lerner Publications Company
A division of Lerner Publishing Group, Inc.
241 First Avenue North
Minneapolis, MN 55401 USA

For reading levels and more information, look up this title at www.lernerbooks.com.

Main body text set in Aptifer Sans LT Pro.
Typeface provided by Linotype AG.

Library of Congress Cataloging-in-Publication Data

Names: Fishman, Jon M., author.
Title: Hockey's G.O.A.T. : Wayne Gretzky, Sidney Crosby, and more / Jon M. Fishman.
Other titles: Hockey's GOAT | Hockey's greatest of all time
Description: Minneapolis : Lerner Publications, 2020. | Series: Sports' greatest of all time | Includes bibliographical references and index. | Audience: Age 7–11. | Audience: Grade 4 to 6.
Identifiers: LCCN 2018044377 (print) | LCCN 2018046190 (ebook) | ISBN 9781541556331 (eb pdf) | ISBN 9781541555990 (lb : alk. paper)
Subjects: LCSH: Hockey players—Canada—Biography—Juvenile literature. | Hockey players—United States—Biography—Juvenile literature.
Classification: LCC GV848.5.A1 (ebook) | LCC GV848.5.A1 F58 2020 (print) | DDC 796.962092/2—dc23

LC record available at https://lccn.loc.gov/2018044377

Manufactured in the United States of America
1-46055-43471-1/25/2019

CONTENTS

During a face-off, hockey players race to gain control of the puck. They need to be fast and accurate when the puck is dropped by the referee.

FACE-OFF!

Have you ever talked with your friends about your favorite hockey players? Do you like to think about what players are the greatest of all time (G.O.A.T.)? Talking about great athletes and comparing their stats is one of the best parts of being a sports fan.

FACTS AT A GLANCE

MARTIN BRODEUR won 691 games in his career. That's 140 more games than any other goalie has won.

MARK MESSIER won six Stanley Cup titles in 11 seasons. Only nine players have ever won more than six Stanley Cups.

GORDIE HOWE was the oldest player in NHL history. He retired at the age of 52.

WAYNE GRETZKY held 61 NHL records when he retired. His 1,963 career assists are more than 700 assists ahead of any other player's total.

But there's much more to think about than stats when making a top 10 list of the best hockey players ever. How can you compare a forward whose job is to score goals with a goalie whose job is to stop them? Comparing players from different eras can be even trickier. The game has changed a lot over the years. From 1942 to 1967, the National Hockey League (NHL) had just six teams. With so few teams, fewer players got a chance to play compared to the modern NHL. The league currently has 31 teams fighting for the Stanley Cup each season.

Hockey equipment has also changed. In the NHL's early years, players didn't wear helmets. In 1979, the NHL ruled that all players entering the league must wear helmets. Helmets, better pads, and other equipment let players focus on the game and worry less about injury. Hockey sticks changed too. Modern stick materials are lighter. Lighter materials allow players to move the stick faster and use less energy.

Despite using heavy wooden sticks of the past, top scorers such as Maurice Richard (*bottom right*) set records that remained unbroken for years.

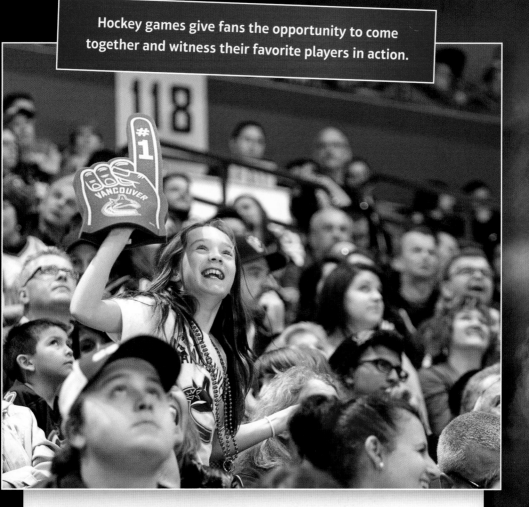

Hockey games give fans the opportunity to come together and witness their favorite players in action.

As you learn more about great hockey players of the past and present, you'll form your own opinions about them. You might even disagree with the order of the players in this book. That's not a problem. In fact, forming your own ideas about the greatest players of all time shows that you're a true hockey fan!

SIDNEY CROSBY

Hockey fans knew that Sidney Crosby was going to be a superstar before he ever hit NHL ice. He began skating when he was three years old. When he was 10 years old, he scored 159 goals in just 55 games. In 2003, he totaled 162 points in 57 games for his high school team. Points are goals and assists combined. The Pittsburgh Penguins

were so sure Crosby would be great that they chose him with the first overall pick in the 2005 NHL Draft.

Crosby proved it was a good decision. In his first season, he finished sixth in the league in points. The next year, he led all NHL players in points. He did it again in the 2013–2014 season. He finished in the top 10 in points each season except seasons when he was injured and didn't play much. Along the way, Crosby led the Penguins to three Stanley Cup championships.

SIDNEY CROSBY STATS

- ▶ Fans and league officials voted Crosby into seven NHL All-Star Games.

- ▶ He won the Hart Memorial Trophy as the NHL's most valuable player (MVP) twice.

- ▶ He won the Conn Smythe Trophy as the NHL playoffs MVP twice.

- ▶ He won the Maurice Richard Trophy as the NHL's top goal scorer twice.

- ▶ He is sixth all time in the NHL in points scored per game.

MARTIN BRODEUR

#9

Goalie Martin Brodeur took the NHL by storm in the 1993–1994 season. He won 27 games that year with the New Jersey Devils. He took home the Calder Memorial Trophy as the league's best rookie. That was just the beginning of Brodeur's incredible career. Over the next 20 seasons, he set all-time records that may never be topped.

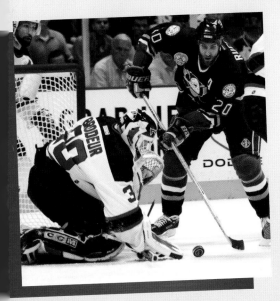

His 691 wins are the most ever for a goalie. No other goalie comes close to matching Brodeur's 28,928 career saves. And his 125 career shutouts set an all-time record. He even scored three goals in his career, a rare feat for a goalie.

Brodeur's personal stats are mind-blowing. He came through for his team where it mattered most: in the playoffs. He has the second most playoff wins for a goalie in NHL history with 113. He also helped the Devils win the Stanley Cup in 1995, 2000, and 2003.

MARTIN BRODEUR STATS

He played in nine NHL All-Star Games.

He won the Vezina Trophy as the NHL's top goalie four times.

He won the William M. Jennings Trophy as the goalie with the fewest goals scored against him in a season five times.

His 24 career playoff shutouts are the most ever in the NHL.

He played more NHL games than any

MARK MESSIER

For most of Mark Messier's 25-year NHL career, he wore a bright letter *C* on his jersey. The letter stood for captain—the team's leader on the ice. Messier's fighting spirit and fierce leadership skills helped make him the most successful captain in NHL history. He's the only captain to win the Stanley Cup with two different teams.

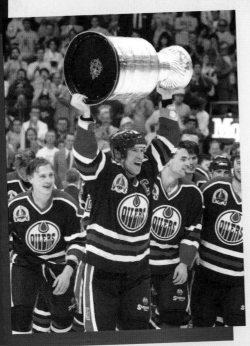

Messier was a tough forward who played with a passion few players could match. He was also an incredibly skilled passer and scorer. He won the Stanley Cup for the first time in 1984 with the Edmonton Oilers. Messier helped the Oilers win it again in four of the next six seasons. Then he joined the New York Rangers in the 1991–1992 season. He led the Rangers to a championship in 1994. That gave Messier six Stanley Cup victories in 11 seasons.

MARK MESSIER STATS

- He played in 15 NHL All-Star Games.

- He won the Conn Smythe Trophy as the NHL playoffs MVP in 1984.

- He won the Hart Memorial Trophy as the NHL's MVP twice.

- His 1,887 career points are the third most in NHL history.

- Both the Edmonton Oilers and the New York Rangers retired his jersey number. No other player may wear number 11 for those teams.

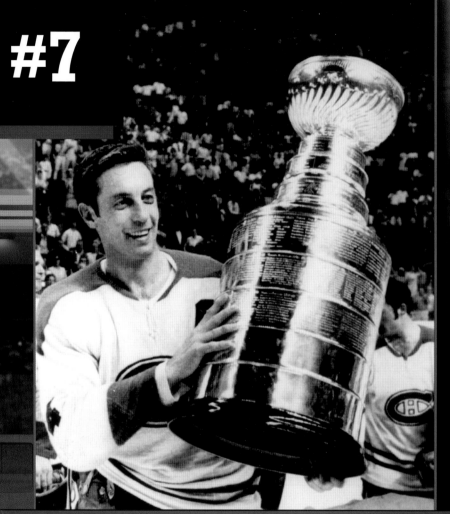

#7

JEAN BÉLIVEAU

At six feet three inches (1.9 m) tall, center Jean Béliveau
was one of the tallest players on the ice. He played for
the Montreal Canadiens in the 1950s and 1960s. His long
legs and smooth skating style made him incredibly fast.
He was also one of the best passers and shooters in the
league. Those skills helped Béliveau lead Montreal to the

longest dynasty in hockey history. In his 18 seasons in the NHL, he and the Canadiens won the Stanley Cup 10 times.

When his playing days ended, Béliveau began a 22-year career as a vice president with the Canadiens. Under his leadership, Montreal won the Stanley Cup seven more times. Teammates and opponents knew Béliveau as a gentleman who always had time to help people. In his honor, Montreal awards the Jean Béliveau Trophy each year to a player who has given back to the community.

JEAN BÉLIVEAU STATS

► His 17 Stanley Cup victories as a player and team official are the most in NHL history.

► He played in 13 NHL All-Star Games.

► He won the Hart Memorial Trophy as the NHL's MVP twice.

► He won the Art Ross Trophy in 1956 as the NHL's top point scorer.

► He won the Conn Smythe Trophy as the NHL playoffs MVP in 1965.

MAURICE RICHARD

His Montreal Canadiens teammates began calling Maurice Richard the Rocket. Soon fans and reporters did too. His shot from his right-wing position was like a rocket streaking toward the goal. And when Richard raced down the ice on his skates, some swore it might have been easier for defenders to stop a real rocket.

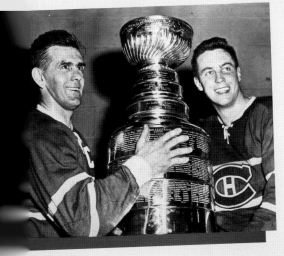

Richard's strength, skill, and fiery style of play were unique. They helped him lead a dynasty in Montreal in the 1940s and 1950s. The Canadiens won the Stanley Cup in 1944, 1946, and 1953. They were just getting started. Beginning in 1956, the team won the NHL championship five years in row. That's something no other team has done. In honor of Richard's incredible career and scoring ability, the NHL began awarding the Maurice Richard Trophy in 1999. The award goes to the league's top goal scorer each season.

MAURICE RICHARD STATS

- He was voted into 14 NHL All-Star Games.

- He won the Hart Memorial Trophy as the NHL's MVP in 1947.

- He led the NHL in goals scored five times.

- He was the first player in NHL history to score 50 goals in a season.

- He was the first player in NHL history to score

#5

BOBBY HULL

Crack! Bobby Hull's mighty slap shots echoed in pro
hockey arenas from 1957 to 1980. Goalies feared them,
and teammates looked on in awe as he scored goal after
goal. His shots often sent the puck soaring at more
than 100 miles (161 km) per hour. And the puck would
often rise or sink on its way to the net, making it nearly

impossible to stop. His slap shots helped him score 604 goals with the Chicago Blackhawks, the most in team history. Hull wasn't just a superstar player. He was also a good sport. He won the Lady Byng Memorial Trophy in 1965 for sportsmanship.

After 15 seasons in Chicago, Hull left to join the Winnipeg Jets of the World Hockey Association (WHA). He brought his incredible slap shot with him. He scored 303 goals in seven seasons with Winnipeg. In the 1974–1975 season, he scored 77 goals. That's the most in WHA history.

BOBBY HULL STATS

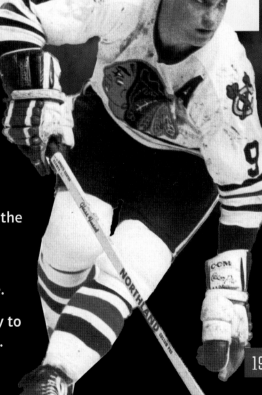

▶ He was voted into **17 NHL and WHA All-Star Games**.

▶ He won the **Art Ross Trophy** as the NHL's **top point scorer three times**.

▶ He won **the Hart Memorial Trophy** as the NHL's MVP twice.

▶ He won the Gary L. Davidson/Gordie Howe Trophy as the WHA's MVP twice.

▶ He was the first player in NHL history to score more than 50 goals in a season.

#4

BOBBY ORR

Defensemen weren't supposed to score. Their job was to stop the other team from scoring by blocking shots and giving painful body checks. But Boston Bruins defender Bobby Orr changed all that. His amazing speed and skill with the puck allowed him to pass and shoot like no defenseman before him. Orr had nine hat tricks in his

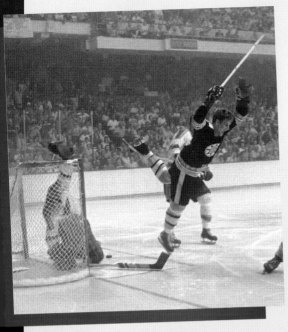

12-year career, more than any other defenseman. In 1970–1971, he set all-time records for his position with 102 assists and 139 points.

Orr was much more than just a scorer. He played a tough defensive game and made it difficult for the opposing team to score when he was on the ice. His fierce defense and scoring were key to Boston's Stanley Cup victories in 1970 and 1972. A bad knee cut Orr's career short at the age of 30. If it hadn't, he could have been the greatest player of all time.

BOBBY ORR STATS

▶ He was voted to play in nine NHL All-Star Games.

▶ He won the James Norris Memorial Trophy as the NHL's best defenseman eight times—more than any other player won it.

▶ He won the Conn Smythe Trophy as the NHL playoffs MVP twice.

▶ He won the Art Ross Trophy as the NHL's top point scorer twice. He's the only defenseman to win the award.

▶ He won the Hart Memorial Trophy three times as the NHL's MVP.

MARIO LEMIEUX

Mario Lemieux's career was filled with firsts. The Pittsburgh Penguins chose him with the first overall pick in the 1984 NHL Draft. He scored a goal with his first shot in his first NHL game. He won the Calder Memorial Trophy as the rookie of the year. Lemieux's size, speed, and shooting were unmatched. Fans and players thought the center had a chance to be the greatest player the game had ever seen.

Lemieux helped Pittsburgh win the Stanley Cup in 1991 and 1992. But health problems often stopped his career. He had broken bones and back surgeries. In 1992–1993, he had a shocking 104 points in just 40 games. Then he learned he had cancer and left the Penguins for treatment. He returned before the end of the season and won the NHL scoring title despite playing 24 fewer games than the player in second place played.

MARIO LEMIEUX STATS

▶ He played in nine NHL All-Star Games.

▶ He won the Art Ross Trophy six times as the NHL's top point scorer.

▶ He won the Hart Memorial Trophy three times as the NHL's MVP.

▶ He won the Conn Smythe Trophy as the NHL playoffs MVP twice.

▶ His career average of more than 1.8 points per game is the second best in NHL history.

GORDIE HOWE

Gordie Howe's hockey career was like no other. It began in 1946 when Howe was 18 years old. In his first NHL game, he scored a goal and got in two fights. Over the decades to come, he kept scoring and fighting. No player in NHL history has quite the same blend of hockey skill and toughness. In 25 years with the Detroit Red Wings, Howe and his teammates won four Stanley Cups.

In 1973, Howe joined the WHA's Houston Aeros. He spent four seasons in Houston and led the team to two championships. Then he spent two years with the WHA's New England Whalers. Howe returned to the NHL in 1979 with the Hartford Whalers and scored 41 points. He was 51 years old at the beginning of the season. It's no wonder that he earned the nickname Mr. Hockey.

GORDIE HOWE STATS

▶ He played in **23** NHL All-Star Games.

▶ He won the **Art Ross Trophy** six times as the NHL's **top point scorer.**

▶ He won the **Hart Memorial Trophy** six times as the NHL's MVP.

▶ He finished in the top five in the NHL in points scored **20** seasons in a row.

▶ When he retired in 1980, he was the NHL's all-time leader in games played, goals, assists, and points.

WAYNE GRETZKY

Fans call Wayne Gretzky the Great One, and the nickname says it all. No player has ruled hockey or any other sport the way Gretzky did in his 20 NHL seasons. Consider the stats. He holds the records for most goals, most assists, and most points in a season. His 1,963 career assists are more than any other player's assists and goals *combined*.

Gretzky was the best player in the game and won four Stanley Cups with the Edmonton Oilers. But he wasn't bigger or stronger than other players. He was rarely the fastest skater on the ice. His greatness came from fantastic hockey skills and an amazing ability to predict the action. He always seemed to know where the puck was going and could get there before anyone else. His passes rarely missed his teammates. His shots were always on target. Gretzky's stats are shocking, and many of his records will likely never be broken.

WAYNE GRETZKY STATS

▶ He played in 18 NHL All-Star Games.

▶ He won the Art Ross Trophy 10 times as the NHL's top point scorer.

▶ He won the Hart Memorial Trophy nine times as the NHL's MVP.

▶ His 2,857 career points are the most in NHL history by almost 1,000 points.

▶ When he retired in 1999, he held 61 NHL records.

YOUR
G.O.A.T.

Now that you've had a chance to read about some of the greatest hockey players of all time, it's your turn to join the action. Do some research on hockey's greatest players. Start by reading some of the books and websites listed on page 31. Talk to adults who have been hockey fans for years, and see what they think. Ask a librarian to point you to other sources of information. Where else can you find out about great hockey players?

Write your list of hockey's greatest players, and ask a friend to make one too. Then compare your lists. Do they match? If not, look at the differences and talk about your opinions. You can make other hockey lists too. Who are the greatest goalies of all time? What are the best teams in NHL history? You decide!

HOCKEY FACTS

▶ When a team wins the NHL championship, each member of the team gets to take the Stanley Cup home. Some players hold parties and take fun photos with the famous trophy.

▶ The fastest slap shot ever recorded zoomed at 110 miles (178 km) per hour. Denis Kulyash of the Russia team in the Continental Hockey League took the shot.

▶ Did you know that hockey pucks are frozen before NHL games? Freezing rubber pucks makes them less bouncy during games.

▶ Modern players are lucky that pucks are made of rubber. Legend says that when hockey was invented in Canada in the 1800s, players used whatever they could find for pucks. They even used frozen cow dung!

GLOSSARY

body check: a block of an opposing player with the body

center: a forward who usually plays near the middle of the ice

dynasty: a long period of dominance by one team

forward: a player whose main job is to score or assist goals

hat trick: three goals in one game by one player

NHL Draft: an event in which NHL teams take turns selecting new players

points: goals and assists combined

rookie: a first-year player

shutout: a game without a goal scored by the opposing team

slap shot: a shot taken by swinging the stick at the puck

wing: a forward who usually plays on one side of the ice

World Hockey Association (WHA): a pro hockey league in North America that existed between 1972 and 1979

FURTHER INFORMATION

Gretzky
http://www.gretzky.com/

Hall, Brian. *Sidney Crosby: Hockey Star*. Mendota Heights, MN: North Star Editions, 2018.

Monson, James. *Behind the Scenes Hockey*. Minneapolis: Lerner Publications, 2020.

NHL
https://www.nhl.com/

Savage, Jeff. *Hockey Super Stats*. Minneapolis: Lerner Publications, 2018.

Sports Illustrated Kids—Hockey
https://www.sikids.com/hockey

INDEX

PHOTO ACKNOWLEDGMENTS

Image credits: Kevin Abele/Icon Sportswire/Getty Images, p. 4; Jeff Vinnick/ NHLI/Getty Images, p. 7; Bettmann/Getty Images, pp. 8, 17 (right), 21 (left), 24, 26; Bruce Bennett Studios/Getty Images, pp. 8, 11 (right), 13 (left), 14, 15 (left), 15 (right), 23 (left), 27 (left), 27 (right); Joe Sargent/NHLI/Getty Images, p. 9 (left); Len Redkoles/NHLI/Getty Images, p. 9 (right); John Giamundo/Bruce Bennett/Getty Images, p. 10; Allen J. Schaben/Los Angeles Times/Getty Images, p. 11 (left); Damian Strohmeyer/The LIFE Images Collection/Getty Images, p. 12; Lawrence K. Ho/Los Angeles Times/Getty Images, p. 13 (right); IHA/Icon SMI, p. 16; Transcendental Graphics/Getty Images, p. 17 (left); Hulton Archive/Getty Images, p. 18; Sovfoto/UIG/Getty Images, p. 19 (left); Archive Photos/Getty Images, p. 19 (right); Focus on Sport/Getty Images, pp. 20, 25 (right); Steve Babineau/ NHLI /Getty Images, pp. 21 (right), 25 (left); Mike Slaughter/Toronto Star/Getty Images, p. 22; New York Post Archives/Getty Images, p. 23 (right); Kirill_Vytovtov/ Shutterstock.com, p. 28. Design elements: Adam Vilimek/Shutterstock.com; Iscatel/Shutterstock.com; conrado/Shutterstock.com.

Cover: Steve Babineau/National Hockey League/Getty Images (Wayne Gretzky); Joe Sargent/National Hockey League/Getty Images (Sidney Crosby).